GREAT ANIMAL COMEBACKS
SAVING THE AMERICAN ALLIGATOR

by Karen Latchana Kenney

PoGo

Ideas for Parents and Teachers

Pogo Books let children practice reading informational text while introducing them to nonfiction features such as headings, labels, sidebars, maps, and diagrams, as well as a table of contents, glossary, and index.

Carefully leveled text with a strong photo match offers early fluent readers the support they need to succeed.

Before Reading

- "Walk" through the book and point out the various nonfiction features. Ask the student what purpose each feature serves.
- Look at the glossary together. Read and discuss the words.

Read the Book

- Have the child read the book independently.
- Invite him or her to list questions that arise from reading.

After Reading

- Discuss the child's questions. Talk about how he or she might find answers to those questions.
- Prompt the child to think more. Ask: American alligators were once on the endangered list. Do you know any other animals on this list? What can you do to help?

Pogo Books are published by Jump!
5357 Penn Avenue South
Minneapolis, MN 55419
www.jumplibrary.com

Library of Congress Cataloging-in-Publication Data

Names: Kenney, Karen Latchana, author.
Title: Saving the American alligator / by Karen Latchana Kenney.
Description: Pogo books edition. Minneapolis, MN : Jump!, Inc., [2019]
Series: Great animal comebacks | Audience: Age 7-10. Includes index.
Identifiers: LCCN 2018022644 (print)
LCCN 2018025543 (ebook)
ISBN 9781641282772 (ebook)
ISBN 9781641282765 (hardcover : alk. paper)
Subjects: LCSH: American alligator—Conservation—Juvenile literature.
Classification: LCC QL666.C925 (ebook) | LCC QL666. C925 K48 2019 (print) | DDC 597.98/4—dc23
LC record available at https://lccn.loc.gov/2018022644

Editor: Jenna Trnka
Designer: Anna Peterson

Photo Credits: Svetlana Foote/Shutterstock, cover; Eastmanphoto/Dreamstime, 1; Eugene Kalenkovich/Shutterstock, 3; tswinner/iStock, 4; Images Etc Ltd/Getty, 5; ClassicStock/Alamy, 6-7; State Library & Archives of Florida, 8-9, 10, 12-13; FLPA/Mark Newman/Age Fotostock, 11; FLPA/Alamy, 14-15; All Canada Photos/Alamy, 16; Arto Hakola/Alamy, 17; passion4nature/Getty, 18-19; brians101/iStock, 20-21 (foreground); THEPALMER/iStock, 20-21 (background); Matthijs Kuijpers/Dreamstime, 23.

Printed in the United States of America at Corporate Graphics in North Mankato, Minnesota.

TABLE OF CONTENTS

CHAPTER 1

HUNTING AN ANCIENT REPTILE

Scales cover this giant **reptile**. It is almost entirely hidden underwater. Can you see it? It is an American alligator.

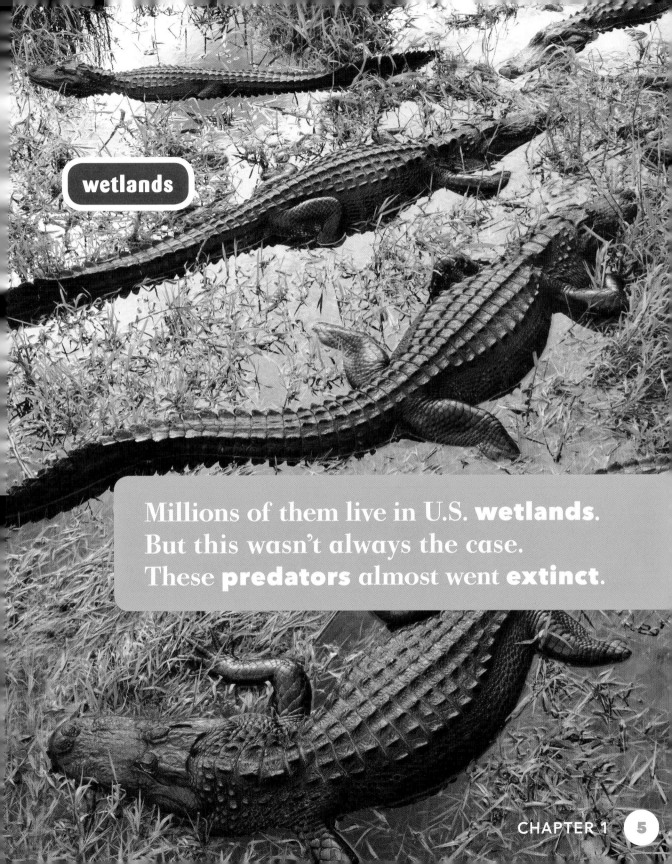

wetlands

Millions of them live in U.S. **wetlands**.
But this wasn't always the case.
These **predators** almost went **extinct**.

alligator skin

Alligators have been on Earth for a long time. How long? Around eight million years! They survived Earth's changing **climate**. And changing ocean levels. What has been their biggest threat? Humans.

Native Americans hunted them first. They ate the meat. They used the skins, too.

DID YOU KNOW?

Alligators haven't changed much over time. Rough scales cover their bodies. They can grow to be 15 feet (4.6 meters) long.

In the 1800s, this reptile's **population** was high. But people kept hunting them. Settlers hunted them for their meat. Skins were used to make shoes and bags. And people moved into their **habitats**.

DID YOU KNOW?

Many alligators were killed during the American Civil War (1861–1865). Why? Soldiers wore boots made of their skins. Horse saddles were made from the skins, too.

CHAPTER 2

SAVING THE ALLIGATOR

By 1960, it was clear alligators were in trouble. **Overhunting** left few in the wild. No laws were in place to protect them.

They were on the brink of extinction. Something had to be done. Some states limited hunting seasons. But populations still did not grow.

State workers **tagged** these reptiles. Why? To track and study them.

Hunting them was made illegal across the country in 1962. They were listed as an **endangered species** in 1967. But **poachers** still killed them. Why? To sell the skins for high prices.

DID YOU KNOW?

The 1967 law led to another. The Endangered Species Act of 1973. It gives states money. The money helps states save endangered animals.

alligator farm

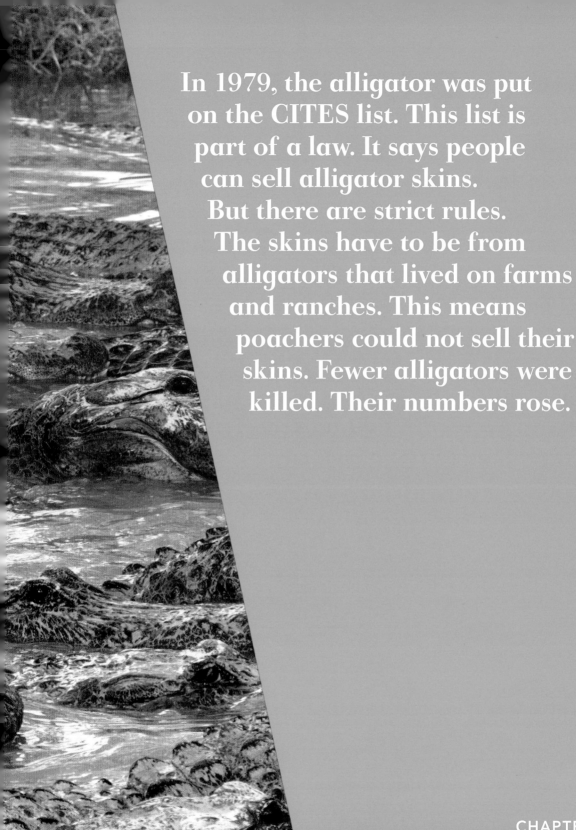

In 1979, the alligator was put
on the CITES list. This list is
part of a law. It says people
can sell alligator skins.
But there are strict rules.
The skins have to be from
alligators that lived on farms
and ranches. This means
poachers could not sell their
skins. Fewer alligators were
killed. Their numbers rose.

CHAPTER 3

ALLIGATORS IN THE WILD

In 1987, the U.S. Fish and Wildlife Service took them off the endangered list. Now you can see them in the marshes and rivers of the South. They **bask** in the sun for warmth.

prey

They hunt **prey**. Birds. Fish. Turtles. Snakes.

Millions live in the wild today. Many are born each year. They can live to be about 35 years old.

TAKE A LOOK!

Where do American alligators live? The southeastern United States. They live in swamps, rivers, marshes, and lakes. Florida's Everglades **National Park** is home to many.

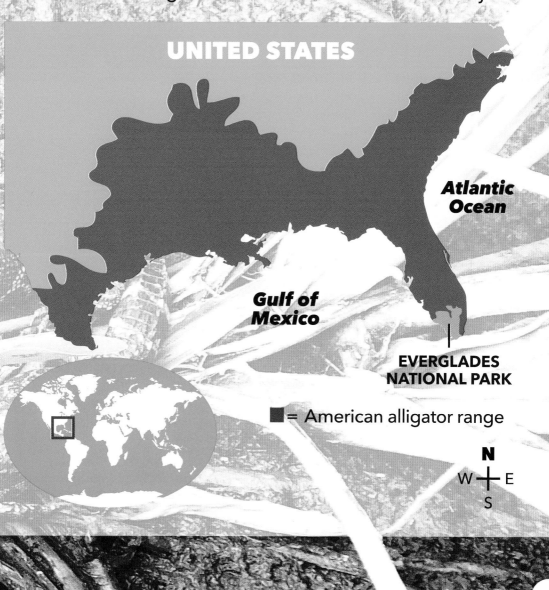

UNITED STATES

Atlantic Ocean

Gulf of Mexico

EVERGLADES NATIONAL PARK

■ = American alligator range

N
W   E
S

Alligators are a **keystone species**. They eat many animals. This keeps the wetlands in balance. They help turtles in the Everglades. How? Turtles keep their eggs warm in old alligator nests.

Losing habitat is now this reptile's biggest threat. People build on the lands where they live. Alligators have made a comeback. But we must still protect them. How can you help?

ACTIVITIES & TOOLS

BUILD AN ALLIGATOR NEST

Alligators build mound nests for their eggs with rotting materials. As they rot, they heat up the nest. This allows the baby alligators to grow inside their eggs. Try making a mound nest, just like an alligator!

What You Need:
- cookie sheet
- leaves
- sticks
- mud
- thermometer
- notebook
- pen

❶ Set your materials up outside. Use the cookie sheet as the base of the nest.

❷ Start with some mud. Place some in a circle.

❸ Add some sticks and leaves. Add more mud. Keep building with these layers until you have a small mound.

❹ Stick the thermometer into the side of the mound. Wait a minute. Record the temperature.

❺ Leave the mound in the sunlight for a few hours. Check the temperature and write it down. Did it change? Check again in a few hours. What happens?

GLOSSARY

bask: To lie or sit in sunshine.

climate: The weather typical of a place over a long period of time.

endangered species: A plant or animal that is in danger of becoming extinct.

extinct: No longer found alive.

habitats: The places and natural conditions in which animals or plants live.

keystone species: A species of plant or animal that has a major impact on and is essential to the ecosystem in which it belongs.

national park: A large section of land that is protected by the federal government for people to visit and to preserve wildlife.

overhunting: Hunting an animal excessively to the point that the animal becomes scarce.

poachers: People who hunt animals illegally.

population: The total number of something living in a certain area.

predators: Animals that hunt other animals for food.

prey: Animals that are hunted by other animals for food.

reptile: A cold-blooded animal that crawls or creeps on short legs and reproduces by laying eggs.

tagged: Placed a device in or on an animal to track its movements and behaviors.

wetlands: Marshy and wet areas of land.

INDEX

TO LEARN MORE

Finding more information is as easy as 1, 2, 3.

❶ Go to www.factsurfer.com

❷ Enter "savingtheAmericanalligator" into the search box.

❸ Click the "Surf" button to see a list of websites.

FACT SURFER